At the Other Side of the Ocean

Julie Pujol-Karel
Lulu Press Inc.

A few words from the writer:

It is my joy to present my fourth book, to my family and friends and to all the readers that have appreciation for the art of poetry.

I take this opportunity to give thanks to
Mr. Andres Puello, founder of Festival Hispano del Libro in Houston. He gave me the opportunity to present my first work to the public *"Imposible Olvidar"* in that great event.

Equally, I want to give thanks to
 Mr. Tony Diaz, founder of "Nuestra Palabra" and organizer of "Houston Latino Book & Family Festival" where I was able to present to the public my second book *"Impossible to Forget"*.

To my friend that unselfishly has guided me with all the information necessary to publish my work, author and writer Marie Delgado Travis.

To the editor, my dear daughter
Janett Pressley-Baxter, she in addition brings this project to a final phase so you can have a quality and professional book in your hands.

To my sister Célida Pujol-Leon responsible for the book cover.

But above all, my dream is a reality because "Everything is Possible with Him" Luke 18:27.

At The Other Side of the Ocean

This book is dedicated to the memory of all the Cubans that have drowned in the ocean attempting to reach USA; and to those that were valiantly fortunate enough to arrive.

The Media has given very little publicity to the constant pain and agony lived by these people and their relatives here in the main land and elsewhere. The number of Cubans that have lost their lives on the stretch from Cuba to Florida in search of liberty is incalculable; attempting to escape the Communist regime imposed by the Castro brothers on the island. They have made an incredible sacrifice risking their lives navigating the open sea on handmade rafts.

Although the great majority of Cubans don't make it to safety, they all have taken a great risk. This clearly spells the inhumane conditions that the Cubans have been exposed to live through the years under the communist regime of Castro.

It touches me deeply, because I have a nephew (Roberto Carballo) that had no other choice than to escape from Cuba in a homemade raft. He drifted on the ocean for five dark nights and days before he made it to safety "At the other Side of the Ocean".

Table of Contents

At the Other Side of the Ocean

At the Other Side of the Ocean

At the other side of the ocean
What is there?
Greenery, freshness, peace,
A road without impediments to walk by,
A hope of light that allows you to embrace
The most beautiful dreams you dare to have.

At the other side of the ocean
What is there?
Sadness, uncertainties, necessities,
They are deprived of the most elemental things,
Food, medication, hope, and liberty.

At the other side of the ocean
A wide ocean separates us.
It holds the secrets of lives that never made it.
Their dreams drowned and died in search of liberty.

Oh! My raft brothers...
I feel so sad!
So many lives have been lost,
They could never arrive,
To the free land,
To the other side of the ocean
To the sea shores.

Bello
(Beautiful)

Bello! Infinitely Bello –
As a calmed, green ocean.
Brave, as the tempestuous ocean itself.

Bello! He offered gallantries with every awakening,
encouraging, sharing his love, and his wisdom
with others in his path.
He always saved the tenderness of a kiss,
and a warm embrace for his gal.

I remember many instances of our life -
But one occasion had come alive.
An evening we spent at Julian,
seated on a mountain peak, the sky,
a veil of shining stars for scenery.
The stars seemed so close that I felt I could leap to touch
them.

The evening was cool although it was summer time.
He covered my shoulders with a shawl,
it was not enough,
then he covered my body with his to keep me warm.

Bello! Infinitely Bello –
As a flowering garden on springtime.
But the road that he traveled had a set of double doors at the
end.
Curiously enough, he entered alone one day,
because alone we are born.
He never returned!
Now his body is laid to rest covered by snow each winter,
waiting for resurrection day far away from me.

Time! It is your best friend and your worst enemy as well –
It passes by merciless, leaving a flavor of bittersweet
memories.
OH! Silly me, again I was taking a ride through my memories,
remembering things of my past.

While doing so, I discovered that I own a treasure,
a chest filled with priceless memories.
You know? The chest is not for sale.
You would not care to buy my troubles anyways.
You would not care to walk the path I walked so long ago.
There were many things that I don't care to share...
Inside the same old chest from where these beautiful
memories had come alive today.

Oh! Bello, infinitely Bello -
A love, that was mine once.
Now it is tucked away forever in my memory.

Coffee for Two

Seated outside on the swing this morning,
sipping my first cup of espresso coffee, I thought of him.
When was the last time we had a cup of coffee together?
Are memories fading?
Or do I prefer not to open the pages
of a book that took me so long to close?

He was not a coffee drinker
or so he said when we first met,
but he got accustomed to having a demitasse of espresso with
me every morning,
before we rushed to work on separate ways.

No – I don't care too much for coffee,
I recall, telling me another day.
But he never lost the occasion to prepare Turkish coffee when
his friends came over to converse.

One Christmas evening –
He had been working at the emergency room
twenty-four hours straight.
Came home with a small gift and excused himself –

I am sorry, I could not go shopping to choose a gift for you.
But I have found something neat in the hospital gift shop
when I took a short break...

It was a black coffee mug hand painted
with a red passion flower and a dainty hummingbird.
Inside the cup a small coffee package "Hazelnut"
my favorite flavor.

Coffee for two in a single mug I asked?
He smiled placing the gift in my hands.
I conserve that old mug, up to this day.

He did not care for coffee or so he said –
But we sipped many cups together,
every morning before we went to work.

I Made My Own Party

I went to the flower shop to buy a bouquet of flowers,
Wrote my address on the envelope, I also added my name.
Please rush the order I said to the counter girl,
I need to be sure that the flowers are delivered today.

I went to the beauty shop so they could tint my white hair,
They did an excellent job,
I thought it is only fair!
I took the opportunity and threw in a pedicure as well.
The massage I could not omit,
While they were serving me, cheese, wine, crackers and
grapes.

I left the place feeling renewed, mind, body and soul-
High spirited as I am though "It is not enough"...

I went to Kohl's department store, looked around for a while,
Then I found a summer dress, I like it, it suits me well!
I got so excited with my flowery dress,
I talked myself into buying a pair of sandals as well,
To show off my pedicure; my nails were painted red.

Then, I had stopped at Randall's, to buy a good wine
Well maybe not too expensive, "I was running low on cash".
I picked up a very small cake, but then I had a change of mind
I took instead ice-cream and apple pie.

By the time I got home, the mailman had passed by,
He had placed in the mail box, mixed with bills and
Advertisements a few birthday cards.
I thumbed through the pile, threw the advertisements away,
Did not open the bills 'cause I had no money left to pay –

I was reading the cards with deep emotion when the door bell
Rang, it was a fellow, to deliver the flowers that I have bought
before.

Oh! The flowers, "what beautiful flowers"
I said to the guy, and the card is it blank?
I almost forgot I have sent it myself,
But it brought me such joy! So just as well.-

Celebrate Julie, celebrate! Listen to the music,
Drink the wine,
Eat the cheese and crackers, ice-cream and apple pie.
Sing alone, dance a song, and elevate a thankful prayer to the
LORD.
Today you are? Oh! I forgot how old.

Harbor Lights

I see the harbor lights, tiny dots glowing at a distance.
Difficult to perceive which ships are coming
to enter the wharf or which ones are departing to open sea.

My heart continues to wait patiently in dismay,
for the return of a ship,
one that sailed, furrowing the ocean long ago
taking my dreams as cargo and never returned.

I wait, feeling the cool breeze of the San Francisco Bay on my
bare shoulders.
This August evening, teenagers roller skate
holding hands.
"Puppy love" I guess.

While I sit on an old iron bench feeding the birds,
Seagulls and Doves are keeping me company.

Yet, my eyes are set on the horizon,
trying to visualize the ships entering the harbor,
looking for the return of a vessel that carried my dreams away
a long time ago.

The harbor lights are flickering far away...

Autumn of My Mind

It's still hot in Houston,
90 degrees yesterday-
It dropped to 68 at night,
but this early morning it is hot again.

The flamboyant trees had begun to undress.
While the sage continues to hold fast,
to its purple dress of flowery tassels.

Leaves begin to fall and dance with the wind,
flying free at last off the branches
that kept them captive all summer.

The pine needles have covered the front lawn
of my neighbor's house.
As I walk by, the falling leaves salute me,
swirling with the wind, engulfing me,
as if the leaves wanted me to stay, inviting me to dance.

No – I cannot stay,
I have to walk away and continue my journey.
There is so much to see!

The birds are singing loudly and free
flying from branch to branch.
Are they imitating the leaves?

There is autumn in my mind,
although it continues to be
90 degrees in Houston.

Paper Balls

Papers, paper balls!
How many I have now on the floor?

Muse – Are you on strike?
Or did you get jealous when I wrote some short stories?

Please come back...
I would like to write poetry again,
Even, if I never rhyme.

My words flowed at ease before,
As flower buttons open in spring.

My mind travels empty now,
I cannot concentrate,
The lines are not flowing
I am a wreck.

Paper balls, paper balls,
Countless pieces are now on the floor.

Life Goes On

Life goes on and we have to live –
We must be happy, lucky that we breathe.
Death is a part of the package received when we are born.
We don't wish to confront it and yet we know...
As we are born one day, equally one day we will go.

Although we are aware of this reality,
We know it is a fact and the way it will be.
No one wishes to see his or her beloved one depart,
For a world that is unknown,
(Except for what it is taught in the Bible).
So I hold fast to that teaching,
Otherwise, it is not worth living.

We breathe each day and we keep on going –
Your heart constricted by pain,
If you have lost someone due to death.

But nothing can be done except:
To keep on PRAYING, to keep on LIVING.
Smiling, enjoying what you have.
Contemplating nature and its wonders at best,
Remembering always those that went ahead of you to a new
place.

Life goes on and we go forward,
Celebrating with joy when a child is born.
Although we know he also comes with the same package,
One day he will see how we also go.

"The chain is broken" – I have said to my sister –
A few of us have departed...

"DON'T BE AFRAID" this separation is temporary.
One day! The chain will be completed again,
When we also leave from here to HEAVEN.
We will be together forever...
In a world that is NEW and DIFFERENT.

Note: Even death can be a positive experience if you know
where you are going.

Rodin

Everyone talks about Davinci's Mona Lisa.
Michelangelo lives through the "Sistine Chapel".
Incredible paintings describing humanity from our beginning
to "Judgment Day"-

But I admire Rodin: "The Thinker"-
He is my favorite sculptor,
He was great.

He received the commission to paint
"The Gates of Hell"
Divine Comedy of Dante.

By the master hands the figures came alive.
Each one has a story to tell.
"The Thinker" – Was himself,
Very muscular, filled with strength.

He was never able to finish his commission,
Thinking of each character the time he spent.

He sculpted "Adam"; He made "Eve" –
Then he sidetracked to "The Kiss".

The Kiss-The story tells that Francesca's father arranged her
marriage.
She fell in love with Paolo, the messenger, and the groom's
brother.
Both died by the dagger of the brother's hand.
Rodin captured the tenderness of their
"Eternal Kiss" forever.

"Eternal Spring" – Where lovers touch faces with tenderness.
"Eternal Idol" – Only the lips touch gently the delicate skin.

Oh Rodin! – Strong thinker, how I admire your work:
"The Cathedral", "Nude Balzar", "Danaide", "Mask of Sorrow",
"Burghers of Calais" on and on...

But what a Master Piece I see in your famous sculpture
"Hand of God" – It is holding humanity in his hands.

A Part of Me

A part of me wishes to reach heaven
On this quiet morning of "Valentine's Day"
I wish that I could talk with him
To share the good news:
My second book is done at last.
It has a lot of him, of my eternal love
It seems he is alive in many pages.

He did not suffer of an illness called "Jealousy"
He always felt secure of himself
When I wrote of past romances
I recall he used to say: "don't deny it, it is o.k."
The book of life has many pages it is made that way.

He was the muse for my new pages
The reason he is in my book today
but he went away one day
filling new pages with sorrow and pain.

Today I am alone, ruminating in silence of days that went by,
I dare to ask myself a question,
Could I love again?
In solitude I respond to self
No – never again

Souvenirs

Today, I move alone, among souvenirs
that I have collected through the years.
As I unpacked, I have added a few more to my collection.

There is no anger in my heart.
No, I feel no anger, toward the man who left one day our
beaches, and went back to his roots,
to his country, thinking it would be for a short while, but he
never returned.

There is no anger in my heart,
although, he took mine with him.
I have tried to find that part of me, ever since.

He left it scattered among the oceans,
the valleys, the forest,
wherever he took it along with him.

So, I continue to travel
adding new souvenirs to my collection,
while trying to collect the pieces,
of my shattered heart.

A Guiding Light

I saw the light, the golden crown –
I heard the noise of fluttering wings.
I saw the white dove encircling my surroundings
A halo of light illuminated me.

I felt energized with new goals and desires,
After feeling sand dunes crushing my soul for so long.
Enlightened with new purposes my spirit awakened
To the song of a dove.

I am not a fanatic but it is not a coincidence,
That I was meditating a few hours before,
The Lord came to me in the form of a dove.
Energizing my soul as he has done before.

Opposite Poles

He enjoys baking, I don't.
I like to eat what he bakes,
Oh! He is so kind,
He brings me cookies and cakes, sometimes.

He grows vegetables, I grow flowers.
He has an orchard; I have a garden filled with flowers.
He brings me squash, tomatoes and bell peppers,
I bring to him roses and daisies.

He loves the woods and lakes,
He is a country creature.
Me? I like the ocean and the seagulls,
I am a city creature.

Opposite poles we are, we know each other's heart.
We share the same concerns,
While the world continues, it changes for the worse.

He is so quiet and polite!
I am so noisy, half of the time!
And he brings me cookies,
And I give him flowers,
He brings me veggies,
And I give him roses.

Ah! We never have discussed politics,
So I don't know which party he favors,
And we don't talk about religion,
Although we say to each other
"God Bless You" sometimes on special occasions.
We hug each other in the middle of the street,
And I don't care what the neighbors, "Might think of me".

Our Darling Angels

Today I sat among a group of Angels –
Mother of pearl the skin,
Blue, Green and Honey Suckle eyes...
Representing the Ocean,
Representing the Sky,
Also the Earth in which we abide.

In the midst of these Angels –
Another Angel came.
Curly dark Brown hair
Cinnamon skin;
Dark Gray shining eyes.

Representing the Moon,
Representing the Wind...
She brings light to our evenings,
Coolness to our lives.

I looked up to the Sky
And felt so grateful...
A deep love and devotion
Bathed my heart and soul.

And I thanked the "Lord"
For the beautiful Angels
That he brought to our home.
Especially for Julianna,
My granddaughter our JOY

The Accident

We both backed-up our cars, at the same time.
We did not see each other; where were our minds?
Our bumpers touched, I heard the crack...
Calm, collected, cool as I could be,
I turned off the motor, and stepped out of the car,
To see if we had damages, or how bad it was.

In front of me stepped a tall, handsome young man.
What are you going to do about it? - Polite he asked -
Ah! We will exchange insurance documents – I answered -
While my poetic mind, was running fast.

Holy cow! "I said to myself"-
This handsome young man ...
Blue/green eyes – he appears to be a "California Guy".
The type of fellow, that goes out surfing, at summer time.

Where are you from? – He asked me -
I was from Cuba a long time ago -
I have lived here three fourths of my life -
But I have kept my accent – It is charming he replied-

Now we were ready to exchange information.
But in the spare of a moment he told me:
"You know, I don't believe that it is worth it" –
As for my car I replied, "I don't worry, it is all banged-up
anyways"-

Mine – He said –"The damage is minor, it is your paint over
mine-
Small, I think that $50.00 will fix it all –Don't you agree?
Yes, I agree, but I have no checks with me to pay you -.
But if you trust me, I'll put one for you in the mail -.
Yes, it is fine; you can do it in a week or so -.

I gave him my card, He gave me his address.
Oh! My God I said to myself…my poetic mind again was right.
He was from Beverly Hills, California.
His mother lived in San Diego – La Jolla area, like me in a
past time.
We had so much in common! Although I am an old lady and
he is a young man.

You know, it felt like when you find a relative in a faraway
place.
I am so glad I bumped into him.
And resolved the issue "California Style"-

Disguised Angels

You might think that Angels don't exist –
Or perhaps they are above in the infinite,
look around and you will see,
"Angels do exist".

They are not celestial being of light
with feathered wings.
They are not silhouettes, dressed in organdie,
they could be people like you and me.

Look around...
Can you see them?

If someone extends you a hand when you are in need,
if someone gives you a hug when you feel sad...
If someone cheers you up with a word of hope,
You can be assured that "An Angel spoke".

Don't be unkind or unfriendly when you are in a rush –
Be friendly and warm as you can be.
Because you don't know when
an Angel is passing by.

I have found more than once
"Angels disguised".
Some were wearing t-shirts, and a pair of jeans,
a skirt, a blouse or a fancy suit.

I am so glad that I have worked with you.
Cause I have found in many of you
"Disguised Angels" helping me.

The Dance

Through all stages of my life I have danced.
During difficult times and through good ones too -
I danced through all my chapters from a very young age.

In my early childhood I danced **Ballet.**
I grew up, and I was not allowed to dance it anymore.
(The tutus were too short) and father said no, no.

When I was a teenager I danced **Tango.**
When my father saw me, it came to a halt.
I recall what he said:
"If I ever catch you dancing to that rhythm again
A convent will be your new living place".
Oh! Poor Mother she was to be blamed.

Quickly I stopped and learned the **Rock and Roll**-
But that type of dance so crazy and wild...
He also said **NO, NO.**
When my father saw me he virtually died
"You can't do that"! For sure you will get a heart attack.

But I have danced through all the stages in my life
In difficult times and also the good times.
I danced the **Waltz, slow danced and the cha-cha-cha,
The Hip-Hop, the Twist,**
and whatever else came along my way.
it helped me to keep in shape.

Father is gone –
I am very old.
But I will keep on dancing
Until the day I'm gone.

A Potluck

I don't like the kitchen except for perking coffee,
To make sometimes sandwiches, and to serve me some wine.
I don't like the kitchen, I don't like to cook
But I love to eat all sorts of food.

I like to taste food from different cultures,
A connoisseur,
I have eaten in many restaurants across the Globe.
But if I invite my friends to eat at home
You can rest assured it will be a pot-luck.

As for my share, I'll buy the food from a restaurant,
and go to Sam's Club for an apple pie.

When my friends comment that the food is great,
I close my mouth not to give myself away.
And when they ask me to share my recipe,
I reply smiling "I can't do that" it is a secret from the family;
my ancestor's recipe.

Mm, Mm, Mm!

Mm, mm, mm! Blueberry muffins in the oven,
Mm, mm, mm, the coffee is perking on the counter top.
Bacon is sizzling on the saucepan,
The aroma of the food has awakened me.

I got my feet into the slippers
And said a prayer rapidly,
Grabbed my robe and rushed out of the bedroom
To where the aroma was coming from.

Mm, mm, mm! My sister is up.
Her face is clean, she wears no make-up,
She combed her hair with her usual pony-tail
She wears a t-shirt, what else is new!
Oops! She forgot to wear her pants,
But her feet are covered with a pair of socks,
Darn, it is so cold!

What prompted you to get up so early? –
Today is Sunday, don't you know!
I wanted to sleep in this morning
But as you can see I could not.

Why not? She answered –
I made no noise to wake you up.
No, my sister you have not –
But the aroma of the Blueberry muffins,
The perking coffee, the bacon sizzling on the stove,
Has awakened up my senses and I have wakened-up.

Mm, mm, mm! It was worth the sacrifice,
Of an early rise on this cold morning.
Thank you for breakfast and espresso coffee.

To: My sister Aleida.

Only the King

Kingdoms rise and fall –
Kings comes and go.
They sign treaties that don't last.
They talk of peace but they do war.

But there is a kingdom soon to arise.
A kingdom that will remain forever.
The King of Kings will be our King
The PEACE HE will bring is everlasting.

Until that day there will be no PEACE
As much as we are wishing for it.
Only HE can bring the PEACE,
The HARMONY and LOVE that we are seeking
For so long without results.

Return to Texas

I never thought I'll be back again –
To the place where I begun a life of freedom.
I never thought that I'll return
Or hear the thunders roar.

Here I am –
I did not plan it this way.
But I am so glad to see these plains,
The greenery of it grasses
The cattle grazing throughout the land
To see and feel the falling rain,
In the land where I begun to live again...

Cami

Twirling in the living room of her mother's friend house,
She dances – The dance of the seven veils in her young
imagination.

The other children, surround her clapping.
Although it is not her birthday we are celebrating,
She is the center of the attention.

Her black and long hair, flies while she dances,
It shines at the contrast of the dimmed chandelier's light,
forming arabesques on the wall.

Her pink musseline dress,
Evocates memories of cotton candies sold at a fair long ago.
A large bow tied her diminutive waist on back of her little
dress -
You can imagine angel wings instead while she twirls and
twirls,
Her dance of the seven veils in the living room;
Knowing at her young age that she is
"The Center of Attention"-
Cami...

Baptism

HOLY SPIRIT, come fly low -
Touch the minds of my grandsons.
Put a brand new heart in them,
Fill it with your spirit and your **LOVE.**

HOLY SPIRIT, come fly low...
In the baptismal waters they are now dipped in faith,
May they make wise decisions as they grow.
Bring them up, forever clean.
Fill them now with the **HOLY GHOST.**

May they reach the heart of others for your **Glory.**
May their classmates see the difference in them!
And thirst for the knowledge and the **SALVATION** you impart,
To whom so ever care to ask.

HOLY SPIRIT, come fly low –
Bless forever my grandsons....
Fill them with your immense **LOVE.**
Help them walk the **Christian Walk.**

HOLY SPIRIT, come fly low –
Touch their lives forever more.

Patience is Love

Shawn and Annette meet in High School –
She had fallen in LOVE with him from the beginning of their
friendship.

Shawn had begun to awake to manhood –
He wanted to fly, to try his new wings,
To meet many girls to see how it feels –
He only wanted Annette's friendship.

She was very sure of her feelings for him,
And never let her hopes go.
With patience she thought, I would win his heart –
He will get tired and one day he'll be mine.

Time passed by and after graduation,
The young man of the story became a Navy Man,
To serve his country and his fellow man,
But Annette was always in the back of his mind.

Of course he got tired of running around, he settled his wings.
He changed his view of an old friendship.
A burning desire to be with her was born
And he realized it was there all along.

The Angels are singing above,
Harps in hands they play a LOVE song.
The music is heard in heaven and earth
The bells are ringing for Shawn and Annette.

A Note to Father

A guitarist, a writer, a poet,
He has raised six daughters with the help of the Lord.
A wise man, patient and trust worthy.
He had always guided us with good judgment and sincerity.

His years gave him the experience he needed,
The Lord gave him guidance to teach us what was right.
He made a great effort to raise all of his daughters
Nothing ever lacked in the peaceful home.

Today with love and devotion,
I dedicate this poem to him, to the kind man that gave me life.
Because by his teaching,
today I am not just a small woman,
But somebody, that helps mankind and society
Always ready to lend a hand.

One Day We Shall Be With You

The Lieutenant has departed
He was kind, loving, and our sunshine.
Loved by those who knew him
Respected by his fellow man.

My dear father...
Loved life in such a way
That he never thought the years passed by.

A soul filled with youth.
Never missed an opportunity to share a joke,
To make you laugh.

He had the privilege to live a long healthy life.
A good husband, perfect father,
Excellent brother and a true friend.

Finally the years took its toll,
His old body gave up.
He left on a trip to see new places,
Different landscapes, the unknown.

Mounting on eagle wings
His soul flew to the sky
We will see him again one day
He will make us laugh.

Victoria

Tears of JOY streamed down to my cheeks
When I saw this morning the "News Update".
The pictures, the JOY reflected on the faces
of those that surrounded YOU.

The family picture "It is out of series"
and the **"INVISIBLE GUEST"** is also in it;
He is reflected on the faces of each one of you.

You can truly say it:
"GOD HAS SEEN ME THROUGHT IT".

His hands, WORKED behind THE SCENE–
Behind the hands of the Doctors and nurses.
Behind the visitors that came to cheer you up,
behind the kindness of the cleaning lady.

He fluffed your pillow many times,
Covered you with the blanket,
He gave you rest in the middle of the storm,
The will to live and the strength to carry on.

This early morning and in your behalf
To the LORD I have sung my praises!
Because he answered the prayers of us all,
You know "we were driving him crazy"...

Today I see the **"VICTORY IN JESUS"**
For Victoria my young friend,
I am so glad your health is back
Because **you** kept the **FAITH.**

Dream

I want to share with you a fairy tale,
I want to take you with me where I was.
You know, it was very early
Dawn barely awaking.
The aroma of the strong coffee,
At the alcove arrived.
I wanted to sleep again but the rooster sang...
Then, I decided to rise with the dawn.
I went to the vestibule! So early!
Already a farmer with his straw hat,
Mounted the wagon.
The peacocks opened their plumage,
They also greeted the dawn.
The sun beginning to shine
It burned the dew that morning.
Between the green leaves of the trees,
Could be seen the sweet white mangoes
I ran toward the tree
I wanted to take some of the fruits
To share it with you
"Sister of my soul"
More, I woke up abruptly to the noise of the traffic,
That constantly happened under my window.
I remained with empty hands,
The peacocks were not either.
I woke up from that enchanted dream,
The place in my childhood we always visited –
Do you remember my dear sister where I was?

Note: The dream relates to the property "Los Mangoes"
A farm owned by my maternal grandparents. I used to
go and spend vacations with my sister.

Tomorrow

As I wake-up tomorrow, I shall open my window,
the sun will look at me smiling,
Its luminous rays as dawn draws' near
Clearly it will tell me a new day is near.

Rapidly I will come down the stairs,
I will run to the garden to salute the flowers.
The birds will salute me with their chirping songs,
happy that they have new nests
built in the branches of the huge green tree,
that gives shade to my garden.

Oh how beautiful is nature that's created by God's hands!
I am ecstatic of its beauty.
The wind caresses my face, while I listen softly the murmur of
a brook
passing by behind my home.

When I listen to the harmonious set
The bird singing, the wind and the water at the brook, running
so gently,
It is then, that I realize with clarity
that Christ speaks to me through the miracle of spring.

Clouds

The clouds can paint masterpieces upon the sky
Creations made with the constant changes,
Of the sun and specters of light.

Across the sky, the paint brush
On the invisible hand of GOD,
Create with clouds
Whatever you wish to visualize.
And thus I call that type of clouds
"The playful ones".

But when the sun decides to hide,
And GOD is provoked to anger
Another type of clouds shows up
I call those "destroyers".

When the clouds get dark,
It is a sign of madness,
Provoking winds, and hurricanes,
That man cannot control.
Devastating cities destroying farms,
Killing everything on their path

Such was the case not long ago
I hope you still remember.
That day when the clouds opened their windows above,
It brought despair, devastation to New Orleans in 2005.

Persistence

Don't ever lose your faith to reach your goal,
Age does not matter.
Be persistent, fight for your dream,
Otherwise your life will be Incomplete.

What have you dreamed of becoming?
A guitarist, a writer, a poet,
A musician, a singer, a pianist,
A psychologist, a physician,
A teacher, an attorney...
Whatever the case might be.

I met a woman that graduated from a university at age 60.
From life's university she graduated at age 30.
The lady became a widow,
She was left with three children;
She lost her husband in one of those bloody fights,
He tried to eradicate Communism.

Do not blame life circumstances
We are never too old to reach our dreams, our goals.
Whatever you truly want to become
Strive for it...

The Color Green

The color Green is meaningful to me,
By this I don't mean to associate it
With money or with a dollar bill.
Many people will make that connection, but not me.

The color Green I associate with the coming of the spring.
When the trees are awakening showing off their brand new
leaves,
And the grass brown and brittle,
Is transformed to a lush carpet of Green.

The color Green is meaningful to me:
It announces that "Easter Sunday" is approaching.
Death and life is celebrated,
The LORD is living proof of this mystery,
That he resolved at CALVARY.

He was in darkness for three days,
But after that he was resurrected,
I do believe that the color Green has a very special meaning
New hope is born in each spring when nature brings
"LIFE"again.

Stormy Night by the Lighthouse

Darkness fell around the area,
it was not the darkness that the night brings
when the stars and the moon are not shinning above,
but the darkness produced by blackened clouds on a stormy
night.
Rolling thunders, lightening arrows
lighting the sky and the area,
as knives cutting the impenetrable black veil intermittently;
not as the light of shooting stars traveling fast on a clear
evening.

How can the wind transform from a gentle breeze
to a fierce partner of destruction?
Interfering with the peace of the magical night
transforming the calm to storm,
lifting, scattering branches as feathers,
erasing the footprints that were on the sand
of lovers that were kissing earlier,
and of children that were playing.

The miracle of all on the midst of the stormy night
was the persistent beam of light,
The light that emanated from the lighthouse,
Remained majestic, unwavering
Providing a silent warning and guidance
to the ships anchored a shore,
and to all the ships attempting to sail
into the danger of a stormy night.

White Stallion

The White mane flies freely,
It's fast galloping leaves an eco behind.
Hoof prints on sand,
erased by the tide and the wind.

Drink, Steal, Swear, and Lie

I was traveling across the country,
Reading a book at peace...
When a woman sitting next to me,
started a conversation.

Annoyed with the intruder that summoned my attention,
insisting in sharing with me, the rules by which she lives,
I had no choice but to pay attention.

Four things you need to follow to lead a happy life,
I have always done so and I am living right –

Drink, Steal, Swear and Lie:

She probably read on my face,
My dismay and my disgust.
But she immediately added: "Please don't jump into
conclusions".
"Be wise, take my advice".

DRINK: From the everlasting cup, it is a fountain of health
and wisdom.

STEAL: Time to converse with the Lord, he is always waiting
to listen.

SWEAR: You will try to be better today,
by helping others in need.

LIE: If you must, but don't forget the one that laid down his
life for you and do give thanks to the Lord for what he did
for you and me at CALVARY.

After the conversation I felt sorry for thinking bad,
And I had learned my lesson

Don't be quick to jump to conclusion,
Don't judge,
Be patient and listen to others.
The same word has different meanings
How you apply it makes the difference in the story.

Saint Patrick's Day Limerick

All dressed up in green
With clover leaves,
Drinking at the pub, eating mustard greens
They could not leave
Neither me, the best party I had ever been.

Dear Sister

Sadness lays heavy in my heart,
My dear sister you are leaving this earth,
And there is nothing I can do for you,
Except to keep you company in your final days.

The time we spent together was always fruitful.
But it was so brief!
So much left unsaid, so much left undone;
The clock kept on ticking and stole away our time.

I know you have to go,
Although I love you so,
I don't want to be selfish; I can't hold you any longer.

The days are going by, I can't bear to say goodbye...
I am going back home, I can't bear to see you go.

II

Oh! My dear sister: You waited until my return,
I guess you wanted to see me again.
Then trying to be brave after our last embrace,
I asked you – Do you want anything to drink?
In a whisper, half way there half way here you replied:
"Yes my dear, espresso coffee strong as I like it...

*Note: From my hands she sipped her last espresso,
Closed her eyes and she went to join the host of Angels
Three days after this conversation.

Friends

The friends I grew up with,
They left the country as I did.
One went to Italy, three of them to Venezuela
(These three got caught again in the misery of a communist regime).

The friends I grew up with,
They have no country but they are free.
A few went to Spain, and ten to Puerto Rico,
Paradisiacal Island that looks so much like mine,
But with a great difference, it is a part of this land.

The good friends I grew up with,
The majority lives in Miami, California and New York,
I have been blessed enough to keep in touch.

The friends I grew up with,
A few on them were left behind.
(Were trapped in the web of communism),
They don't remember **how it feels to be free.**
They have lived behind invisible iron gates for so long...
They don't have a clue how it feels to be free any more.

The friends' fortunate enough to leave as I did,
They have traveled errands throughout the world.
We left behind our childhood stories
To continue our life, creating new stories.
Each one of us have embraced new friendships,
In the **LAND of LIBERTY.**

Tucked away, inside of each one heart's,
The things we did together remained alive:
The places we went while growing up,
The school, the park, the ice cream parlor,
The movie house, our own backyards.

The old neighbors are now dead and gone,
As well as our parents that came along with us.
Our houses, time has destroyed,
(For lack of paint, lack of materials to repair the properties),
It is the sad part of our stories.

But I am very fortunate to be here,
With FREEDOM of RELIGION and of SPEECH,
Writing as a Poet, expressing what I please.

Imprints

Traces of tiny feet across the white carpet,
Prints of muddy little shoes, across the kitchen floor,
Two different sizes, all in one accord.

The cry of the older
Cause the younger took his favorite toy away,
The cry of the younger
Cause the older has pushed her and fell.

Imprints in my memory, Imprint in my heart,
I'll never forget those pages of my life.
But the footprints are gone from the carpet and the floor
time took care of that!
Now she wears #8 and he #11 ½.

The babies' cries are gone,
It has turned into conversations,
Questions and answers going on both directions.

Imprints in my memory, imprints in my heart
I don't change those treasures,
For gold, silver, or wine.

As time has passed, a circle was completed,
Each one of my angels had two kids
Totaling in all, four sets of footprints.

A pair belongs to the girl, the only one,
She stole my heart away the day when she was born,
Cinnamon is her skin, curly hair and honey eyes.
Bright, kind, tender and sweet, she is the apple of my eyes.

The other three pairs belong to the boys,
These kids are true blessings in my heart and soul.
The first of the three boys, the one with pearl skin,
He is quiet and soft spoken, kind as anyone can be.

The other two are very restless, always busy and inventive,
They have their days, but they are real fun,
And although they are responsible for greater messes.
I would not change them for treasures of this world.

As you can see many years are gone
but I have continued to mop
Footprints on the floor...

Lily the White Bright Cat

My son has a white cat, sweet as she can be –
Fluffy as cotton balls, playful as a child.
But you need to be careful with "Lily the Cat"
If you allow her she will eat no less than six times.

Her blue eyes are so pretty,
Soft looking and loving
She doesn't cry with tears,
Her eyes distill honey.

Lily the Cat: Be careful with her or she takes over!
Gently and quietly she walks to the pillow situated on the
floor,
She looks around and proceeds to clean her claws.

Stealthily she looks to her surroundings,
She sees if she was caught in her mischievous behavior,
Then with guile she takes over the chair,
Her tongue at work for her morning self cleaning,
Leaving behind more hairs flying than the one her owner has
on his head.

She jumps to the couch as if she is the owner,
As if she is the only one with rights to sit on it.
Oh no, you cannot move her away from the couch,
She moans, and growls and she scratches you too.

There is a legitimate reason behind her behavior:
Lily the fluffy cat likes to watch TV
As you and I.

Mother's Day 2008

It is Mother's Day, although we live in two different
dimensions
I am on earth and you somewhere in the firmament.
The love for you thus far from diminishing,
Has grown enough to reach the cosmos
To tell you MOTHER how much I love you.

Conversing with You:
I like to share I am a grandmother as you were once one too.
When you departed I had only a grandchild,
She was a year old the day you said goodbye.

Ever since the family has grown,
I am not the grandmother of one but of four.
The beautiful little girl that was only one when you went home
To be with the Lord, soon will be fifteen and we will celebrate,
To continue the tradition that from you I had learned.

But in preparation for this great day I can't help to remember
The fourteen years since you went home.

I love you MOTHER and I always will
I'll remember you as long as I live.
I remember your aroma of nardos and roses
I remember your voice, I remember your hands
Always sewing dresses for my sisters and me.

I remember you with your apron in the kitchen,
Cooking for us, and the guests,
A little extra went in the pots to give a plate to the beggar
That came by every evening as far as I can remember.

You also made dessert so fine!
Marmalades, pudding breads, milk desserts
And Gods knows what.
My sister, being the rascal that she was,
would eat them all, even hot, in a twinkle of an eye.

Summarizing the conversation today:
I remember your kisses; I remember your embraces,
Did you ever get mad?
I hold no remembrances of that.

Note: This poem won a 1rst place at Spring Fling 2008 – "The
Alamo Family Award"

Tracking Back to Memory Land

It was 1962 – When my eyes saw snowflakes falling gently for
the first time.
Ever since- I have seen the miracle of snowflakes falling,
But the emotion I felt the first time could not be replicated.

The flakes fell on a Christmas Eve,
My first Christmas away from home,
We had no money to exchange gifts,
My Sisters and Me.

But the Lord sent our ways,
That Christmas Eve a priceless gift
The surpassing joy to see the first time
Snowflakes falling.

It covered the roof of the houses,
It covered the trees and the streets,
Although we did not have a coat, boots, gloves or hats,
We went out to touch it, my Sisters and Me.

When we awoke the following morning
The sight we saw by the window pane,
Stuck to my mind in such a way,
That I could paint the scene again if I were a painter.

The weeping willows were crying,
tear drops of ice,
The lake was a solid glass.

Tracing back to my memories
I had gone to Abilene,
To the eve when I saw by the first time in my life
snowflakes falling,
It all took place on Christmas Eve,
My first one in the USA and the coldest!

The Road Taken
Julie Pujol-Karel

Parody of: The Road Not Taken

By Robert Frost

TWO roads converged in a black wood,
I am not sorry because I can travel both
Being a traveler tired and old, I did not stand long
And I looked up to see if the end was close
To where it was flat on the overgrowth.

Then took the other, close enough,
Having perhaps the same bad fate,
Because it was dusty and not traveled well;
Though I have tried not to pass by
There both were different no question asked.

In both the night equally lay
Without leaves or grass had trodden hard,
Oh, I kept the second for a day or two!
Although they both lead to different places,
I am sure one day I will return.

Everywhere youth and youth hence:
Two roads converge on the black wood, and I ...
I took the one most traveled by,
And of course it did not make a bit of difference.

The Healing Power of Music

A serenade, calms your nerves, it brings you joy unsuspected,
if you never expected that gift, yourself esteem will surely
raise.

Soft music returns the balance to your body, to your inner
soul.
Will make you dream, it will take you to places that you have
not visited before.

Salsa music makes you move to the rhythm of bongos.
When your body turns loose,
for sure you will feel the benefits of sweat glands at work.
Your system will be cleansed sweating impurities that your
body held,
as the sweat increases and the pounds are shed,
you will feel better and all your joints will work.

Gospel music "what a gift",
brings to you unsurpassable benefits.
It brings you hope to keep on living.
It frees' your inner person of guilt and shame,
renewing your strength.

Music: Simply is a free prescription for healing; body, mind
and soul.

Who Will Rescue My Heart?

I go out daily but I live in confinement,
I know new faces, but continue remembering only one.
I see other eyes shining full of sexual desire inviting me to live,
to love again.
But I only wish for those others...
Those beautiful eyes that were closed one day and never were
opened again.

At night, I go out alone,
I walk to where the electric lights can not interrupt the light
that emanates
from the stars and the moon on the firmament.
Watching the infinite sky, I elevate a prayer, trying to find
him, vane intent...
By which one of the celestial windows will he show his face?
But nothing, I see nothing, only chimeras, wishful desires of
my broken heart.

Again I leave when dawn is born, in search for other faces,
a characteristic, a glance, a human smile
resembling a little to the dreamed face that this soul of mine
longs for.
I return home, hurt, tired, empty not encountering what I was
looking for.

Who will rescue my heart?
I have uselessly looked for it to no avail.
No one can fill the emptiness that he left one day.

II

I open the coffin loaded with memories;
experiences accumulated through the passages of time.
I see him, I have invented him again.
I kiss him and I feel him on the air that caresses my body,
And in the alcove, when I touch his old pillow,
Thus it mitigates the pain, nailed deep and intense in my heart
and soul.

I walk the streets trying to forget, but cannot encounter
forgetfulness.
I go away to the beach – His surfboard no longer exists.
His candle was extinguished in a glad summer day,
Although for me it was the saddest summer that ever existed.

My silence shouts to him…Why? Why did you go away?
And I want to believe that I hear his voice,
His answer to soothe my pain:
"No, no, I have not left you love of all my torments"
I am with you,
Can you sense me in the soft wind?
In the air that you breathe?
Have you not realized it my love?
I live, in your heart and soul…

Driver

Limerick:

Do you think they can drive any faster?
They do speed as if the road is a spree way,
They blow the horn as if they are a snow mover.
Rolling down the window they scream and gesture ...
"Old Folks go faster"

Golden Age?

"The Golden age" – There is not such, Copper is its value,
you can't stretch your money any more.
Life is that way "a true dilemma".

Before, you had the gold and no time to enjoy it.
Now, time is what you have at hand
but you lack the money to enjoy it.

This is the reality: Gasoline cost much more than diamonds,
An exorbitant commodity that you can no longer afford.

The Social Security that you have paid through the years
To receive benefits when you have reached "The Golden Age"
is not enough to buy a cup of coffee.

Conversing to myself I said: "Be patient", a just man is never
abandoned.
See the other side of the coin some people are worse off.
Go ahead, turn on your light bulb and start using your brain,
I am sure you will find solutions to your problems, think,
think.

Look: Find a lame horse, so it can take you slowly to the
grocery store; place on it a saddlebag to bring your groceries
the old fashion way,

Let the horse eat the grass, in your lawn and your backyard,
Not only have you saved on gas but on the gardener's bill,
Continue to think my friends in ways you can save some
money.

Look: Travel has become expensive, especially on airplanes,
Turn the TV on the travel channel I hope you'll see it my way,
Thus you can go even to Japan without purchasing a ticket
Use your imagination...

If you wish to go to the beach but you lack the gasoline,
Don't make a big deal if you can't and use your imagination:
Fill the bathtub with warm water,
Bring the palm tree from outside, place the same over the
toilet.
Bring the radio inside the bathroom; be sure you listen to
salsa with maracas and bongos.

Don't forget to drink your rum with a peppermint leave,
Start enjoying your life as long as you can breath.
Forget about any pain and also the lack of money
I always do as I want using my imagination.

Recognitions

Houston Literacy Latin Woman of the year -2009
Hispanic Book Fair – Writers Recognition - 2009

Centro Poético Madrid España - 2009
 "La Barca Vacia" " The Empty Raft"

Tenth Annual International Latino Book Awards
Book Expo - Los Angeles CA - 2008
Best Poetry Book "Imposible Olvidar" 2nd Place.

Millennium Press – Publishing grant
 Assistance to the Hispanic Writer
for poetry book "Del Otro Lado del Oceano" 2008.

Poets Northwest -21th Annual Spring Fling
The Alamo Family Award – 1st Place for" Mother 2008"

League of American Poets – 2008 – Poem "Dream".

Centro Poético Madrid España – 2008
¿Quién Rescatara Mi Corazón? Who will Rescue my Heart?

Poets Northwest - 19th Annual Spring Fling 2006 – Poems for Old Lovers.

First Place for "Look for Me".

Third Place for "Memories".

Poetry Society of Texas – Houston Chapter - Winter Poetry Festival – 2005

The HAP Fulgham Award - First Place for "Shells".

Lucidity Poetry Journal Award –Second Place for "Mourning".

<u>Southwest Writers Club</u> – (Writing Competition) – 2005

First Place for "The White Rose"- "La Rosa Blanca".

Third Place for "Castro"- "Poem of a Sad Land".

Houston Poetry Fest – 2004

University of Houston/Houston Art Endowment.

Juried Poet – for "Exilio" "Exile".

<u>Southwest Writers Club</u> - (Writing Competition) – 2004

First Place for "Memories".

Second Place for "You are My Light".

<u>Southwest Writers Club</u> - (Writing Competition) – 2003

Publications in Anthologies:

2008 – The Long and Short Anthology
        Poem "Tomorrow"
2008 - Inspirations - League of American Poets –
        In My Dreams.

2008 – White Oaks Press - Dreams

2006 – The Long and the Short of It – Poets Northwest.
        Poems - "Rodin" y "A Guiding Light"

2006 – Windows - University of Houston – Alvin Campus.
        Poem – "Big Bear Lake".

2006 – Laberinto de Sentimientos -Centro Poético – Madrid,
        Poem – "Esta Noche".

2006 – Miradas de Nostalgia - Centro Poético – Madrid,
        Poem –"Amor de Siempre".

2005   Aurora   Centro Poético – Madrid, España
        Poem – "Cruz Liviana".

2005 – The Arts Alliance Center – Clear Lake, Texas
        "Exhibition by the Square Foot"
        Poems Exhibited -"Shells", "Memories" and "You Are
        My Light"
        "Art by the Square Foot" Chap Book.

        2005 – Houston Poetry Fest – Outbound Series –
        Webster, Texas

        Juried Poet – Poems – Fate, Danube River, Opposite
        Poles, A Child at the Astros's Dome, New Orleans
        Tragedy.

2004 - Houston Poetry Fest (Nineteenth Anniversary)
       Juried Poet - Poem – "Exilio" "Exile".

2004 – On the Wings of Poetry – (Lavender- Aurora)
       Poem "When Years Go By".

2004- Poems of the World – Palatine, Illinois
       Poem – "Returned to the Lord" autumn

2004- Poems of the World – Palatine, Illinois
       wPoem – "Look for Me #2" spring

2003 - Poems of the World – Palatine, Illinois
       Poem - "Look for Me #1

Member of Poetry Society of Texas – Houston Chapter and
Northwest Chapter.

Invited often by "Nuestra Palabra" radio program sponsored
by The Arts and Literacy of Houston, station KPFT, Tuesday
7:00 PM, and also by the local radio station 920AM program
"Entérate" from 1:00 PM to 2:00 PM, and also, to Christian
Radio, Rocky Mountains, Colorado, Saturday morning.

Directs and participates in Poetry Jam for "The Hispanic Book
Festival" – Annually, in February - Houston, TX.

Founder of "Conversing through Poetry" a poetry group that
met   at Barnes & Noble Copperfield Store/Northwest
Houston, Texas. The group meeting place now is:
at a Public Library, Bear Creek Branch, Katherine Tyra.

Founder of Millenium Literacy group, meeting at :
Bayland Community Center, Houston.

This book can be obtained at:

http://stores.lulu.com/juliepk

www.Amazon.com

Barnes & Noble
www.barnesandnoble.com
Borders
www.borders.com
www.Lulu.com

And all major book stores by request.

Books published by the author:

1. Imposible Olvidar -2007
2. Impossible to Forget – 2007
3. Del Otro Lado Del Océano – 2008
4. At The Other Side of the Ocean – 2009

Made in the USA
Monee, IL
07 July 2026

56550167R00042